WITHDRAWN

602611

MAE JEMISON
Space Scientist

By Gail Sakurai

CHILDRENS PRESS ®
CHICAGO

602611

DEDICATION

*For Nicholas and Cameron —
follow your dreams.*

PHOTO CREDITS

Cover, 1, 3, 4, 7, NASA; Courtesy Stanford News
Service; 12, 13, UPI/Bettmann; 14, 15 (all three
photos), 17, 19, 20, 21, 23 (both photos), 24, 26, 27, 28,
NASA; 29, 31, AP/Wide World; 32, NASA

EDITORIAL STAFF

Project Editor: Mark Friedman
Design and Electronic Composition: Biner Design
Photo Editor: Jan Izzo

Library of Congress Cataloging-in-Publication Data
Sakurai, Gail.
    Mae Jemison, space scientist / by Gail Sakurai.
        p. cm. — (A picture-story biography)
    ISBN 0-516-04194-0
    1. Jemison, Mae, 1956–   — Juvenile literature. 2. Afro-
American women astronauts—United States—Biography—
Juvenile literature. [1. Jemison, Mae, 1956–   . 2. Astronauts.
3. Women—Biography. 4. Afro-Americans—Biography.]
I. Title. II. Series: Picture-story biographies.

TL789.85.J46S25 1995
629.45′0092—dc20
[B]   95-3814
                                                                           CIP
                                                                            AC

THREE . . .

Two . . .

One . . .

Liftoff!

The space shuttle *Endeavour* thundered into the morning sky above Kennedy Space Center. Higher and higher it soared over the Atlantic Ocean. A few minutes later, *Endeavour* was in orbit around Earth.

The space shuttle Endeavour *lifts off.*

Aboard the spacecraft, astronaut Mae Jemison could feel her heart pounding with excitement. A wide, happy grin split her face. She had just made history. She was the first African-American woman in space. The date was September 12, 1992.

But Mae wasn't thinking about dates in history books. Her thoughts were of the wonder and adventure of space travel. "I'm closer to the stars —

While in space, the Endeavour *astronauts pose for a portrait.*

somewhere I've always dreamed to be," Mae said during a live television broadcast from space.

Mae's dream didn't come true overnight. It happened only after many long years of hard work, training, and preparation. Her success story began nearly thirty-six years earlier, in a small town in Alabama.

Mae Carol Jemison was born on October 17, 1956, in Decatur, Alabama. While she was still a toddler, Mae and her family moved to the big city of Chicago, Illinois. Mae considers Chicago her hometown because she grew up there.

Mae was the youngest child in her family. She had an older brother, Charles, and an older sister, Ada. Her parents, Charlie and Dorothy Jemison, were helpful and supportive of all of Mae's interests. "They put up with all kinds of stuff, like science projects, dance classes, and art lessons," Mae said. "They encouraged me to do it, and they would find the money, time, and energy to help me be involved."

Other adults were not as encouraging as Mae's parents. When Mae told her kindergarten teacher that she wanted to be a scientist, the teacher said, "Don't you mean a nurse?" In those days, very few African Americans or women were scientists. Many people, like Mae's teacher, couldn't imagine a little black girl growing up to become a scientist. But Mae refused to let other people's limited imaginations stop her from following her dreams.

Mae loved to work on school science projects. She spent many hours at the public library, reading books about science and space. On summer nights, she liked to lie outside, look up at the stars, and dream of traveling in space. Mae was fascinated by the real-

Mae had always dreamed of becoming an astronaut. Her dream came true in 1987.

life space flights and moon landings that she watched on television. Mae Jemison knew that she wanted to be an astronaut. Although all the astronauts at that time were white and male, Mae wasn't discouraged.

Science and space were not young Mae's only interests. She also loved to dance. Mae started taking lessons in jazz and African dance at the age of nine. By the time she was in high school, Mae was an accomplished dancer, and she frequently performed on stage. She was also skilled at choreography, the art of creating a dance.

In 1973, Mae graduated from Chicago's Morgan Park High School,

Mae at Stanford University

where she was an honor-roll student and excelled in science and math. That fall, Mae entered Stanford University in California. At Stanford, she specialized in African and Afro-American studies, and chemical engineering. Mae continued her dancing and choreography. She also became involved with student organizations, and she was elected president of the Black Student Union.

After receiving her Bachelor of Science degree from Stanford, Mae enrolled at Cornell University Medical College in New York. She had decided to become a doctor. Medical school was demanding, but Mae still found time to participate in student organizations. She served as president of both the Cornell Medical Student Executive Council and the Cornell chapter of the National Student Medical Association.

Mae traveled to several countries as part of her medical training. She studied medicine in Cuba. She helped provide basic medical care for people in rural Kenya and at a Cambodian refugee camp in Thailand.

Mae received her Doctor of Medicine degree from Cornell University in 1981. Like all new doctors, she served an internship, a period of practicing under experienced doctors. Mae completed her internship at the Los Angeles County/ University of Southern California Medical Center. Then she started working as a doctor in Los Angeles.

Although she had settled into a career as a doctor, Mae wasn't finished traveling yet. She remembered the trips she had taken during medical school, and she still wanted to help people in other parts of the world. Mae decided to join the Peace Corps, an organization of volunteers who work to improve conditions in developing nations.

Mae spent more than two years in West Africa. She was the Area Peace Corps Medical Officer for Sierra Leone and Liberia. She was in charge of health care for all Peace Corps volunteers and U.S. embassy employees in those two countries. It was an important responsibility for someone who was only twenty-six years old.

"I learned a lot from that experience," Mae said. "I was one of the youngest doctors over there, and I had to learn to deal with how people reacted to my age, while asserting myself as a physician."

When her tour of duty in the Peace Corps was over, Mae returned to Los Angeles and resumed her medical practice. She also started taking advanced engineering classes.

Mae had not forgotten her dream of traveling in space. Now that she had the necessary education and experience, Mae decided to try and become an astronaut. She applied to the National Aeronautics and Space Administration (NASA), which is responsible for U.S. space exploration. After undergoing background checks, physical exams, medical tests, and interviews, Dr. Mae Jemison was accepted into the astronaut program in June 1987. She was one of only fifteen

Mae was working as a doctor in this Los Angeles office when NASA selected her for its astronaut program.

Mae sits in the cockpit of a shuttle trainer.

people chosen from nearly two thousand qualified applicants!

Mae didn't let success go to her head. "I'm very aware of the fact that I'm not the first African-American woman who had the skills, the talent, the desire to be an astronaut," she said. "I happen to be the first one that NASA selected."

Mae moved to Houston, Texas, where she began a year of intensive training at NASA's Johnson Space Center. She studied space shuttle equipment and operations. To learn how to handle emergencies and deal with difficult situations, Mae practiced wilderness- and water-survival skills. Survival training also helps teach cooperation and teamwork. These are important abilities for astronauts who must live and work together for long periods in a cramped space shuttle.

Mae and her survival-training classmates watch a demonstration of how to build a fire.

Mae in training (clockwise from top): clinging to a life raft in water-survival training; learning to use a parachute; practicing with the shuttle escape pole for emergency bailouts.

15

Mae took lessons on how to move her body and operate tools in a weightless environment. On Earth, the force of gravity keeps us from floating off the ground. But in space, there is less gravity, so people and objects drift about. Since there is no "up" or "down" in space, astronauts don't need to lie down to sleep. They can sleep in any position. To keep from drifting while asleep, they zip themselves into special sleeping bags attached to the shuttle's walls.

During training, Mae got a preview of weightlessness. She flew in a special training jet that simulates zero gravity. The jet climbs nearly straight up, then loops into a steep dive. This is similar to the loop-the-loops on many roller coasters. For thirty seconds at the top of the loop, trainees feel weightless. Their feet leave the floor and they can fly around inside the padded cabin.

Mae and astronaut Jan Davis (left) hold onto each other in NASA's "zero-gravity" training aircraft.

At the end of her training year, Mae officially became a mission specialist astronaut. "We're the ones people often call the scientist astronauts," Mae explained. "Our responsibilities are to be familiar with the shuttle and how it operates, to do the experiments once you get into orbit, to help launch the payloads or satellites, and also do extravehicular activities, which are the space walks."

In the 1970s, NASA designed the space shuttle as the first reusable spacecraft. A shuttle launches like a rocket, but it returns to Earth and lands on a runway like an airplane. A space shuttle has many uses. It carries both equipment and people into space. Astronauts aboard a shuttle can capture, repair, and launch satellites. Shuttles are often used as orbiting laboratories, where space scientists conduct experiments in a zero-gravity environment. In the future, space shuttles might transport supplies and workers for building space stations.

Although Mae was a full-fledged astronaut, she still had to wait four more years before she went into space. While she waited, Mae worked with the scientists who were developing experiments for her mission. She also trained with her fellow crew members. In her spare time, Mae liked to read,

18

This illustration shows how the space shuttle looks during flight. The cargo bay holds Spacelab, the science laboratory where Endeavour's astronauts conducted most of their experiments.

travel, ski, garden, dance, and exercise. She also enjoyed taking care of Sneeze, her white, gray, and silver African wildcat.

On September 12, 1992, the long wait was over. Space shuttle *Endeavour* perched on the launch pad like a great white bird waiting to take flight. Everything was ready for the liftoff.

Mae awoke early to shower and dress. She ate breakfast with the other astronauts. Then, Mae and the crew put on their orange space suits and

The Endeavour *crew on their way to the launch pad*

Mae prepares to board the shuttle.

boarded a van for the short drive to the launch pad. For two-and-a-half hours until liftoff, they lay on their backs, strapped into their seats, as the countdown progressed. At 10:23 A.M., precisely on time, *Endeavour* lifted off on its historic space journey.

Dr. Mae Jemison earned her place in the history books as the first African-American woman in space. Mae said,

"My participation in the space shuttle mission helps to say that all peoples of the world have astronomers, physicists, and explorers."

Endeavour's mission was devoted to scientific research. Mae was responsible for several key experiments. She had helped design an experiment to study the loss of bone cells in space. Astronauts lose bone cells in weightlessness, and the longer they stay in space, the more they lose. If too many cells are lost, bones become weak and can break easily. Scientists hope to find a way to prevent this loss. Mae explained, "The real issue is how to keep people healthy while they're in space."

Mae investigated a new way of controlling space motion sickness. Half of all astronauts experience space sickness during their first few days in

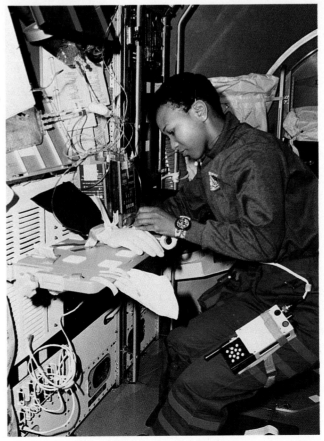

Above: Mae and Jan Davis conduct a zero-gravity experiment. In space, a person's fluids shift toward the upper body. The device Mae is wearing simulates normal gravity and forces the fluids back to the lower body. Left: Mae injects liquid into a mannequin's hand. She is testing new medical equipment that is specially designed for a weightless environment.

23

Mae is all wired up for the biofeedback experiment.

space. They often feel dizzy and nauseated. Astronauts can take medicine to control space sickness, but the medicine can make them tired.

To carry out the space-sickness experiment, Mae had been trained in the use of "biofeedback" techniques. Biofeedback uses meditation and relaxation to control the body's functions. Mae wore special monitoring equipment to record her heart rate, breathing, temperature, and other body functions. If she started to feel ill, she would meditate. She concentrated intensely on bringing her body back to normal. The purpose of the experiment was to see if Mae could avoid space sickness without taking medication. The results of the experiment were not conclusive, but space researchers still hope to use biofeedback in the future.

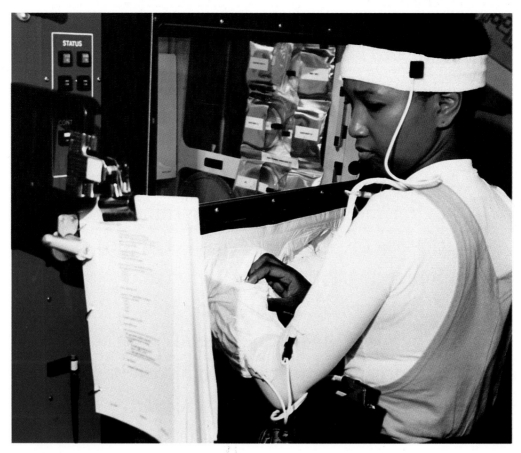

Mae works with the frog experiment.

Mae was also in charge of the frog experiment. Early in the flight, she fertilized eggs from female South African frogs. A few days later, tadpoles hatched. She then watched the tadpoles carefully. Her goal was to find out if the tadpoles would develop normally in the near-zero gravity of space. "What we've seen is that the eggs were fertilized and the tadpoles looked pretty good," said Mae. "It was exciting because that's a question that we didn't have any information on before."

The Endeavour *crew at work*

On September 20, 1992, at 8:53 A.M., *Endeavour* landed at Kennedy Space Center. The crew had spent more than 190 hours (almost eight days) in space. They had traveled 3.3 million miles and had completed 127 orbits of Earth!

Home again. Endeavour *lands on the runway at the Kennedy Space Center.*

Mae with Morgan Park High School's principal, Earl Bryant, at a special homecoming ceremony in her honor

After her space mission, Mae returned home to Chicago. Her hometown welcomed her with six days of parades, speeches, and celebrations. Then she went to Hollywood to accept the American Black Achievement Awards' Trailblazer Award for being the first African-American woman in space. In 1993, Mae was inducted into the National Women's Hall of Fame in Seneca Falls, New York.

Mae Jemison had made her childhood dream come true. She was ready for new challenges. A few months after her space flight, Mae took a leave of absence from NASA to teach and to do research at Dartmouth College in New Hampshire. Then, on March 8, 1993, she permanently resigned from the astronaut corps.

Mae formed her own company called The Jemison Group, Inc. The Jemison Group's goal is to develop ways of using science and technology to improve the quality of life. Mae's company makes a special effort to improve conditions in poor and developing countries.

The company's first project used satellite communications to provide better health care for people in West Africa. Mae also established an international summer science camp for young people.

Mae encourages youngsters to follow their dreams. She is shown here with thirteen-year-old Jill Giovanelli, the winner of the International Peace Poster Contest.

Besides her work with The Jemison Group, Mae spends much of her time traveling around the country, giving speeches, and encouraging young people to follow their dreams. Mae Jemison believes in the motto:

"Don't be limited by others' limited imaginations."

MAE JEMISON

1956   October 17 — Mae Jemison is born in Decatur, Alabama
1973   Graduates from Morgan Park High School in Chicago, Illinois
1977   Graduates from Stanford University
1981   Graduates from Cornell University Medical College
1983-85   Serves in the Peace Corps in West Africa
1985-87   Works as a doctor in Los Angeles, California
1987   Becomes an astronaut
1992   September 12 — Lifts off aboard space shuttle *Endeavour*, becoming the first African-American woman in space
1993   Resigns from NASA to form The Jemison Group, Inc.

INDEX

ABOUT THE AUTHOR

Gail Sakurai always wanted to be a writer, ever since she learned to read as a child. She planned to have her first book published by the time she was thirteen! However, for many years, other interests and needs interfered with her writing. Ms. Sakurai's childhood dream finally came true when her first book was published in 1994 — only twenty-nine years later than originally planned! The book was *Peach Boy*, a retelling of a traditional Japanese legend.

     Gail Sakurai lives in Cincinnati, Ohio, with her husband and two sons. When she is not writing, she enjoys spending time with her family, listening to classical music, and, of course, reading. She is a full member of the Society of Children's Book Writers and Illustrators.